THE TRUTH SHALL SET YOU FREE

by
JOHN OSTEEN

Lakewood Church
P.O. Box 23297
Houston, TX 77228

Copyright © 1978 John Osteen

ISBN 0-912631-13-9

BOOKS BY JOHN OSTEEN

*A Miracle For Your Marriage
*A Place Called There
*ABC's of Faith
*Believing God For Your Loved Ones
 Deception! Recognizing True and False Ministries
 Four Principles in Receiving from God
*Healed of Cancer by Dodie Osteen
*How to Claim the Benefits of the Will
*How to Demonstrate Satan's Defeat
 How to Flow in the Super Supernatural
 How to Minister Healing to the Sick
*How to Receive Life Eternal
 How to Release the Power of God
 Keep What God Gives
*Love and Marriage
 Overcoming Hindrances to Receiving the Baptism in the Holy Spirit
*Overcoming Opposition: How to Succeed in Doing the Will of God
                    by Lisa Comes
*Pulling Down Strongholds
*Receive the Holy Spirit
 Reigning in Life as a King
 Rivers of Living Water
 Saturday's Coming
 Seven Facts About Prevailing Prayer
 Seven Qualities of a Man of Faith
*Six Lies the Devil Uses to Destroy Marriages by Lisa Comes
 Spiritual Food for Victorious Living
*The Believer's #1 Need
 The Bible Way to Spiritual Power
 The Confessions of a Baptist Preacher
*The Divine Flow
*The 6th Sense...Faith
 The Truth Shall Set You Free
*There is a Miracle in Your Mouth
 This Awakening Generation
 Unraveling the Mystery of the Blood Covenant
*What To Do When Nothing Seems to Work
*What To Do When the Tempter Comes
 You Can Change Your Destiny

* Also available in Spanish

Please write for a complete list of prices in the John Osteen Library.
Lakewood Church • P.O. Box 23297 • Houston, Texas 77228

THE TRUTH SHALL SET YOU FREE

As you read through the pages of this book, meditate on these Biblical truths. Crown Jesus as Lord of your life. Resist the devil and he will flee from you. (James 4:7)

It is a shame to see people created for fellowship with God who are dominated and bullied by the devil and his demon forces.

When I was young, I attended a country school and I remember a big bully that I had to contend with at that school.

Let me tell you a story about another bully from a country school that I heard about.

There was a big bully in a country school who always took great delight in picking on everyone. He especially liked to pick on someone smaller than he. He would scare them, beat them, mistreat them and annoy them in every way that he could. This was his joy! He was known in all the community as one who bullied everyone that he could.

One day a wiry little fellow saw this big bully standing with a pad of paper and writing on it with a pencil. This wiry little fellow had a lot of courage and would fight a wild cat! He walked up to the bully and asked, "What are you doing?"

This big bully, in his country drawl, said, "I am making me up a list of everybody that I can 'whup' (whip). I'm writing their names on this piece of paper. I've got the names of everybody I can 'whup' in this school down on this piece of paper."

This wiry little fellow got to thinking that maybe his name might be on this list. He reached over and bravely snatched the list out of the bully's hand. He said, "Let me see that paper!"

As he read it, he finally came to his own name. Bristling with anger, he looked at that bully and said, "Why, you have my name on this list! You can't 'whup' me!!! What are you doing with my name on this list??!!"

The big bully just wilted before the daring challenge of this wiry little fellow. He turned pale with fear and said meekly, "Oh. I will take *your* name off."

You know, the devil is going around making up a list of every Christian that he can defeat. He knows who is ignorant of their standing and their rights in the Lord Jesus Christ, and he has their names on his list.

We need to boldly face satan and say, "I see you have my name on your list. You can't defeat me! I'm washed by the blood of Jesus! I am a new creature in Christ Jesus! I have all power over all your power, satan! In Jesus Name I can cast out demons. I am more than a conqueror!"

Do you know what satan will do?

He will turn pale and tremble. He will take his eraser and say, "Oh, in that case, I will take your name off of my list!"

Hallelujah!

We need to keep satan busy wearing out his eraser erasing our names off of his list!

SATAN HAS BULLIED GOD'S PEOPLE LONG ENOUGH!

He has tormented and harassed God's children because they have not known their rights and privileges in Jesus Christ.

YOUR DAYS OF DEFEAT AND DEPRESSION ARE OVER.

Power will come with knowledge!

As you become knowledgeable about the true supernatural power of God, you will rise to victory in every area of your life.

We are in the latter days. Untold legions of demonic powers have been unleashed upon our children, husbands, and wives. Homes are being wrecked. Preachers are under attack and many are falling.

If ever there was an hour that we need to pray for the ministry and all the body of Christ, it is now. We need to love each other.

"Now the Spirit speaketh expressly, that in the latter times some shall depart from the faith, giving heed to seducing spirits, and doctrines of devils." (I Timothy 4:1)

Doctrines of demons and seducing spirits are looking for their prey. A lot of wrong, misleading doctrines are coming into being.

The Bible tells us in John 8:32 that "Ye shall know the truth and the truth shall make you free."

It does not tell us that if we know certain people we will be free. We cannot be personality conscious. Beware of any man or woman that wants to tie you to their ministry to where you have to find them to get all the truth or get deliverance!

A preacher friend of mine told me of this experience. He said that one day a man came to him for counseling. He was concerned as to whether or not he should go to Africa. He told my friend that a person had prophesied over him that he was to go to Africa.

He asked my friend, "Do you think that I should go?"

I asked my friend what he told this man. This is what he told him:

He said, "Well, I do not know if you should go to Africa or not. However, if you do go, my advice to you is to take this person who prophesied over you with you to Africa. The reason I say this is because you can't hear from God for yourself and they will have to be there with you to tell you when to come home!"

Prophecy should always confirm something that God has already spoken to your heart. It should not direct you! It should not cause you anxiety nor put you into confusion.

"He that prophesieth speaketh unto men to edification, and exhortation and comfort." (I Corinthians 14:3)

Let God guide your footsteps as you walk with Him daily through the Word of God. He has said that His Word "is a lamp unto your feet and a light unto your path." (Psalms 119:105)

Jesus said, "Ye shall know the truth and the truth shall make you free!"

What is the truth? "Thy Word is Truth." (John 17:17)

Jesus said, "I am the Way, the Truth and the Life." (John 14:6)

Jesus is the Living Truth!

"Ye shall know the truth and the truth shall make you free!"

You can be free from fear, from demon powers, from seducing spirits, from doctrines of demons, from sickness, and free from all of the power of the enemy.

KNOWLEDGE BRINGS POWER FROM GOD

Hosea 4:6 tells us, "My people are destroyed for lack of knowledge."

Knowledge!

God's people are cut-off for lack of knowledge. It is not inspiration that we need. It is knowledge.

We need Bible knowledge of what we have through the great redemption in Jesus Christ.

That is the reason people are destroyed today. Homes are destroyed. Lives are destroyed. Some people are too indifferent, too irresponsible and unwilling to be taught the Word of God.

God says that you need knowledge. If you have knowledge, you have power. If you have knowledge, you can operate in God. If you are in ignorance, the devil can overcome you and demons can take advantage of you.

God's people are destroyed for lack of knowledge. They need to know the Word of God. When they know the truth—the truth shall make them free!

Mrs. C. Nuzum, whom God mightily used to bless the body of Christ, tells of her life without the knowledge of the truth and then what happened when the Truth set her free. Jesus will do the same for you!

Here are her own words of what satan had done to her: "I was born sick. My mother said that when I was a baby I cried most of the time. I never had any real childhood. While other children ran and played, I sat and talked to the older people. I had rheumatism all my life until the Lord healed me. My arm was so crippled that I could not put it back or up, but it is now free. My knee was so stiff that I could not straighten it, nor go up or down stairs. I can now run a block to catch a car, and my limbs are as supple as those of a girl sixteen. My heart beat sometimes as though it would leave my body and at other times it seemed to stand still. Again it would tremble so it would cause a profuse perspiration. It pained me as though knives were being thrust through it. I can now go to the top of a mountain and not know I have a heart. I have been completely delivered from paralysis of the left side, and can now walk eight miles and feel fine the next day. I have been entirely delivered from constant pain and fever in the head, and from extreme nervous prostration. In my young womanhood, I was reported dead several times, and when I was graduated from school I had to sit down and rest while reading my thesis.

For twenty-seven years I was never one moment free from pain. I would gaze like a charmed bird at a healthy-looking face, and would gladly have given all that I owned if I could have felt for ten minutes as well people seemed to feel. My sufferings were such that I would rather have died than live. I was treated by the best doctors money could secure, and all concluded by saying the same thing, "There is not a sound spot in her to build health upon." My last doctor was a specialist who had been used to raise people from death's door to health. After a long, careful examination he said, "No doctor or medicine can cure you. You will have to die very soon. If you have any preparations to make, do it quickly."

What a shame to me that I had to be forced to take God as my physician instead of choosing Him. But, oh, how gracious He was to receive me and heal me, so that now at the age of seventy-one, I am doing the work of three women and have not lain in bed from sickness for so long that I cannot remember when I did so last. From having no strength, I have come to have the Lord's strength; from constant sickness to have His health; from forcing food just as I did the bitter medicine, I have come to have an excellent appetite, so that I can eat even the plainest food and enjoy it and never fail to eat a hearty meal, and every bite is sweet. Catarrh had destroyed my sense of smell. Now I can enjoy the perfume of the flowers. I wore glasses all the time. Now I use only a little reading glass, but thread my needle and sew without a glass. My sense of taste was so lost that both sugar and salt were as sand. Now, how good all food tastes! My hearing was so nearly gone that people were passing before me before I heard them coming. Now I have ordinary hearing. For two years I scarcely slept at all; now I sleep like a baby. Then I could enjoy nothing; now I have the deepest enjoyment of all the things God gives me and especially Himself, His fellowship, communion, and Word. Truly, 'old things are passed away; behold, all things are become new; and all things are of God.' God did it all, and blessed be His Name forever. I might add that I have worked strenuously three hundred and sixty-five days a year for thirteen years, with only two little vacations, and am in good condition now. When I look back at what I was, and see what I am, it seems incredible."[1]

YOU SHALL KNOW THE TRUTH AND THE TRUTH SHALL MAKE YOU FREE!!!

If there was ever a day that people need to know the Word of God, it is today. You will not be destroyed if you know the Word of God. "You will know the truth and it will make you free."

You, like Mrs. Nuzum, can be free from whatever disturbs and destroys. "Jesus Christ is the same yesterday, today and forever." He loves YOU! He is

[1]*Life of Faith,* by Mrs. C. Nuzum. Gospel Publishing House, Springfield, MO. pp. 11, 12, 13. (1956)

12

present with you right now! He works through His Word. As you continue to read, the Truth of His promises will become alive to you. As this happens, arise to victory! Rejoice in deliverance! Fall at Jesus' feet and worship Him for giving you the desires of your heart!

KNOW THE GREAT REDEMPTIVE TRUTH

Paul saw this great need for knowledge. He prayed, "That the God of our Lord Jesus Christ, the Father of glory, may give unto you the spirit of wisdom and revelation in the *knowledge* of Him: the eyes of your understanding being enlightened . . ." (Ephesians 1:17-18)

Paul prayed that the Church would have the knowledge of the Lord Jesus Christ that is given by the Holy Spirit. If we do not have the knowledge of who Christ is, of what Christ has done for us, and of what took place in the great redemptive plan of God, we are likely prey for the enemy.

"You shall know the truth and the truth shall make you free."

You need to know what Jesus Christ has done for you.

In Genesis chapter three, satan came in the garden and deceived Eve. She and Adam ate the fruit and they fell into sin. The whole human race was plunged into darkness. Adam, who was the god of this world and lord of all creation, gave his dominion to satan.

God said, "I will put enmity between thee and the woman, and between thy seed and her seed; it shall

bruise thy head, and thou shalt bruise his heel."
(Genesis 3:15)

God was saying that a man would come (a Seed of a woman) who would bruise the head—take the crown of lordship off of satan. God would put enmity between the devil and woman.

Let me say this: That is the very reason the devil has hated every woman. The devil has subjugated womanhood in every land where he has power. He has put women on the level of animals. He hates women because through a woman's body came the Seed—Jesus. He hated women before Jesus came. He hates women now. Wherever satan holds dominion, women are lowered. In many places, they are treated like cattle and veiled in secrecy. They have no privileges. Satan especially hates woman because she bore the redemptive Seed of Christ.

Wherever Jesus is preached and uplifted, womanhood is uplifted and crowned with glory and honored.

The Seed of the woman was to bruise the devil's head. To "bruise the head" refers to historic times, when they would bruise the head of a conquered king. They threw him down, put their foot right on his head and took his crown.

One day that Seed came as God had promised. As you well know, His Name is Jesus. He came to humanity as the Seed of the woman.

When the devil confronted Jesus, Jesus overcame the devil with the Word of God.

Jesus did not come to earth to prove that He was satan's Lord and conqueror. He was already the powerful, omnipotent, Son of the Living God. He had dominion over all principality and power. He came to demonstrate satan's defeat!

The Bible tells us that He created principalities and powers. He was co-existent with the Father from the beginning. (John 1:1-3)

He was satan's master when He came into this world. Whatever He did, Jesus did for you and me!

During His earthly life, Jesus defeated the devil with the Bible. He said, "It is written." (Luke 4:4)

When He faced the devil, He cast out spirits with His Word. (Mark 9:25)

He said, "Get behind Me, satan", which means "get out of my sight!" Immediately satan left. He obeyed Jesus. (Luke 4:8)

Jesus said, "Woman you are loosed from your infirmity" and the demon left. (Luke 13:12)

He healed the blind and blind spirits departed. He was sent to preach the Gospel and recovering of sight to the blind. (Luke 4:18)

He was absolute master of satan!

Jesus is a picture of what a new creature is in the righteousness of God. He had absolute mastery of demon powers.

We do not have to tolerate demons and their torment and attacks on our minds and bodies. Jesus, our example, dominated satan!

Jesus took on Himself our sin, our sickness, our curse, our death. (Isaiah 53:5) He took it all in body, mind and spirit!

He became a spiritually dead man. He suffered for you and me. He went down into the dark regions of the spiritual world. He paid the price. He conquered satan. He arose as Victor!

Millions of Christians are trembling in the face of satan and demon powers today. You will know the truth and the truth will make you free!

We do not know all that happened when Jesus left this earth with our sins, sickness and curse and went to the pit of hell. We do have an indication through this revelation:

"Wherefore He saith, when He ascended up on high, He led captivity captive, and gave gifts unto men. Now that He ascended, what is it but that He also descended first into the lower parts of the earth? He that descended is the same also that ascended up far above all heavens, that He might fill all things." (Ephesians 4:8-10)

Jesus went down into the lower parts of the earth and He led "captivity captive"—He led a train of vanquished, conquered foes.

"And having spoiled principalities and powers, He made a show of them openly, triumphing over them in it." (Colossians 2:15)

He disrobed, made naked and disarmed principalities!!

In those days in Eastern cultures, when a captain conquered another king and kingdom, he would put the king in chains. Behind him would be a long row of prisoners in chains. He would lead them back to his own domain. The captain would come back to his king, leading that army of conquered people. The defeated king would be in chains and all the conquered army behind him in chains. He lead this king in chains, disarmed, and totally defeated. Behind him are his captains, his generals and all of his soldiers. They are presented to this king. Here is the proof that the captain has conquered his foe. He has the king and all of his men in chains. He has all of their armor. He proudly displays all of the spoils.

Jesus is the "Captain of our Salvation." (Hebrews 2:10)

The Bible says that Jesus led a train of captives— of vanquished foes. (Ephesians 4:8—Amplified Bible). He disarmed them and made a show of them openly. (Colossians 2:15)

Actually, Jesus went down into the lower parts of the earth, the dark regions of hell. He conquered satan. He put satan's head down and put His foot on it. He took from him lordship of the human race! He took the crown! He took the keys!

He bound satan and all the host of hell. He stripped them of their authority, power and armor. Then, in the spirit world, He led them before all of the angels, all of the host of heaven and before the Heavenly Father.

He paraded them and showed before all the spirit

world that satan was conquered and every demon was conquered. He sprinkled His blood in the holiest of holies and made a show in the spirit world that satan was stripped of his power.

Jesus Christ is Lord!

These are facts. These are indisputable facts in the legal court of heaven.

But "My people are destroyed for lack of knowledge," said God. (Hosea 4:6)

"You can know the truth and the truth shall make you free." (John 8:32)

You can be free from sin, habits, demon power, sickness and all that hurts and destroys. To be free you must know the truth. Jesus makes you free through the truth of His Word. "He sent His Word and healed them." (Psalms 107:20)

THE WORD OF GOD HEALS A WOMAN

When I first received the Baptism in the Holy Spirit as a pastor of a Baptist church in Houston, Texas, I was eager to pray for any and all sick people that I might meet. I carried a bottle of oil with me and rejoiced at the opportunity to anoint anyone with oil and pray for them. I was so overjoyed to know that Jesus would heal today that I shared about his healing power with everyone.

One night I was called to visit a woman who had had a death in the family. She was to leave the next day to go to a distant city for a funeral. So, I went on a cool, rainy night to visit her.

After I had visited with this member of our church for a while and we had a prayer together, I arose to leave. She said, "Wait a minute, Brother Osteen. I have some coffee and cake for you." As she started to get up, she grabbed her knee and groaned in pain.

I asked, "Are you sick? Do you need prayer for your body?" I was always so thankful to find someone to minister to.

She said, "Oh, Brother Osteen, I have arthritis throughout my entire body and I hurt so badly. I've had it for years. Look at my right hand. It is so stiff."

As I looked at her hand, I noticed that between her thumb and index finger it was completely hardened and stiff. She had no movement in that area of her hand.

I said, "Please let me anoint you with oil and pray for you." She consented, so I anointed her with oil and prayed.

She then went to get the cake and coffee and we sat and talked some more. As we got up for me to leave, she grabbed her leg again and groaned in pain. I said, "Oh, do you still hurt?"

She didn't want me to be discouraged. She knew that I was new in praying for the sick and that we Baptists did not know much about healing then. She said, "Brother Osteen, it is not your fault! You did all that you could do. It is not your fault that I still hurt!" Then she said something that gave me the clue to help her. She said, "You know, Brother Osteen, the Lord expects us to suffer some."

I said, "What did you say?"

She answered, "The Lord expects us to bear some of our pains."

Excitedly, I said, "Did you know that Jesus not only bore our sins, but that He bore our sicknesses too?"

She said, "Why, no, I didn't know that!"

As we stood there at the door, I hurriedly took my Bible and turned to Matthew 8:17. I said, "Look! Look! Read what the Bible says!"

She read, "That it might be fulfilled which was spoken by Esaias the prophet, saying, Himself took our infirmities, and bare our sicknesses."

I said, "See, you don't have to bear your sickness any more than you have to bear your sins!"

That Baptist woman began to shout for joy. When she did, it really scared me because I had never seen a Baptist act like that! I said, "What's the matter? What's the matter?"

She said, "When I read that scripture, all the pain went away!" Then she moved her hand and said, "Look at my hand. I can use it. I can use it!"

She was totally healed in a moment of time!

Why? Because she saw the truth of the Word of God and that Truth made her free!

It will do the same for you!

Some people said, "Jesus casteth out devils through Beelzebub, the chief of devils." (Luke 11:15)

Jesus answered in Luke 11:21. He is talking about satan when He says: "When a strong man, armed, keepeth his palace, his goods are in peace."

Then He begins to talk about Himself in verse 22: "But when a stronger than he shall come upon him, (that is when Jesus went to hell after his death) and overcome him, he taketh from him all his armor wherein he trusted and divideth his spoils."

Jesus gave the spoils to you and to me in the family of God!!!

Jesus clearly indicated that is what He would do. It is what He did!

"Forasmuch then as the children are partakers of flesh and blood, He also Himself likewise took part of the same; that through death He might destroy (bring to naught, nullify) him that had the power of death, that is the devil." (Hebrews 2:14)

This truth will get you out of fear. This truth will break satan's power and set you free!

The power of life and death is not in the hands of the devil. Jesus Christ said, "My Father has absolute power of life and death." (John 19:11)

Jesus destroyed and brought to zero him who had the power of death, that is the devil!

Hear this prophetic word by the Holy Ghost. "THUS SAITH THE LORD: MY PEOPLE PERISH FOR LACK OF KNOWLEDGE. BUT GOD WANTS YOU TO KNOW THAT HE HAS RAISED UP A NEW RACE OF MEN AND WOMEN WHO HAVE THE SAME POWER

AND AUTHORITY THAT JESUS CHRIST HAD OVER SATAN. HE BOUGHT IT FOR YOU WITH HIS OWN BLOOD AND HIS OWN SUFFERING. GOD'S PEOPLE HAVE PERISHED FOR LACK OF KNOWLEDGE.

NOW IN THESE LAST DAYS, GOD IS OPENING THE EARS AND THE EYES OF HIS PEOPLE. THEY ARE RISING UP. THEY ARE REALIZING THAT THEY ARE THAT NEW RACE THAT GOD DESTINED THEM TO BE UPON THE FACE OF THE EARTH. THEY SHALL GO FORTH AND THEY SHALL BRING VICTORY ON THE RIGHT HAND AND ON THE LEFT. THEY SHALL NOT BE OVERCOME, BUT THEY SHALL BE OVERCOMERS. THIS TRUTH IS COMING TO ALL THE BODY OF CHRIST THROUGHOUT THE WORLD. THERE IS A NEW REVELATION COMING TO THEM AS TO WHO THEY ARE IN CHRIST JESUS.

RISE UP! RISE UP! RISE UP! FOR THE WORLD IS IN DARKNESS. THEY ARE WAITING FOR THE CONQUERORS TO COME.

YOU ARE THE RACE THAT WILL BRING DELIVERANCE!!"[2]

You are that race, but ignorance will hold you in weakness. It is truth—knowledge—that sets you free.

When you know something, you can act on that knowledge.

---

[2]This prophetic utterance was given at Lakewood Church, Houston, Texas as John Osteen taught on this subject.

"For this purpose the Son of God was manifested that He might destroy the works of the devil." (I John 3:8b)

Jesus came to destroy the works of the devil. Did He fail? No. He destroyed the works of the devil. Our Heavenly Father "hath delivered us from the power of darkness, and hath translated us into the kingdom of His dear Son." (Colossians 1:13)

YOU are delivered!

You have been delivered from the authority and the power of satanic darkness. You are now in the kingdom of light. The greatest fight satan is making today is to keep you ignorant of this truth!

There is arising a group of people who will shake this world. We are entering into new areas of ministry. There will be such a divine flow of the wisdom, love and power of God. There will be thousands delivered because of the great mercy of God in this hour.

Christ has done so much for us!!!

What is the purpose of the great redemptive work of Jesus?

"How shall we escape, if we neglect so great a salvation?" (Hebrews 2:3)

The purpose of this great salvation is that "through the church, the complicated, many-sided wisdom of God in all its infinite variety and innumerable aspects might now be made known to the angelic rulers and authorities (principalities and powers) in the heavenly sphere." (Ephesians 3:10 Amplified Bible)

If the rulers of the spirit world had known all that would be wrought in this great redemption when they crucified Christ, they would never have done it. They did not know what was going on. In fact, they are still stunned!

The great wisdom of God is that God Himself would come in Christ and bear our sins and be Just and the Justifier of those who believed in Jesus!

The darkened, hellish forces, principalities and powers still do not know the extent of this great redemption!

The church should be so endowed with knowledge, power and the Holy Ghost in our day that they will bring a mighty demonstration of the power of Jesus Christ in the earth.

THE CHURCH WILL SHOW DEMONIC FORCES THE WISDOM OF GOD IN THIS GREAT REDEMPTION. IT IS UP TO THE CHURCH TO DEMONSTRATE THIS!

The church of the Living God should rise up in such knowledge and power that they will show satan the wisdom and power of God in the great redemption of Jesus for us. (Ephesians 3:10)

After He was raised from the dead, "Jesus came and spake unto the disciples saying All power is given unto Me in heaven and in earth." (Matthew 28:18)

He said, "Go ye into all the world, and preach the Gospel to every creature. And these signs shall follow them that believe; in My Name shall they cast out devils; they shall speak with new tongues." (Mark 16:15, 17)

You should have a sure knowledge of your ability to handle demons. You have total authority. YOU ARE a new creature in Christ Jesus.

Knowledge sets you free. Do not be destroyed for lack of knowledge. Know the truth and the truth shall set you free!

The first thing Jesus said would follow the new creature was that, "In My name you will cast out demons." (Mark 16:17)

This truth will get your child out of trouble. It will take your heartache away. It will break the power of witchcraft. It will take away sickness. It will break the power of every form of demonic activity.

Jesus was talking about when the Holy Ghost would dwell in the believer. He said, "I tell you the truth; it is expedient for you that I go away: for if I go not away, the Comforter will not come unto you; but if I depart, I will send Him to you. And when He is come, He will reprove (convince or bring a demonstration) to the world of sin, and of righteousness, and of judgement: Of sin, because they believe not on Me; of righteousness, because I go to My Father, and ye see Me no more; of judgement, BECAUSE THE PRINCE OF THIS WORLD IS JUDGED." (John 16:7-11 Amplified)

The prince of this world has been judged and conquered. By the power of the Holy Ghost, you are to bring a demonstration to the world that he is defeated. The prince of this world has been over-come.

Know who you are in Christ and demonstrate your power over satan. Then tell the world that there is a righteousness available to Christians. Tell them that the only sin that will send them to hell is their rejecting Jesus because He is the only Lord.

DEMONSTRATE YOUR AUTHORITY LIKE THEY DID IN THE BOOK OF ACTS

How did this truth work in the New Testament church which started in the Book of Acts?

The early church did not talk much about the devil. THEY JUST DEMONSTRATED THE TRUTH OF HIS DEFEAT!

Actually, they did not pay much attention to the devil in the Book of Acts which is our church pattern for believers today.

Now you cannot just ignore the devil and think that he will go away. You must realize your authority in Jesus. Martin Luther told a story of awaking in the night. As he lay in bed, he opened his eyes to see that the devil himself stood in the room. In the calm assurance that the "Greater One dwelt within him," he said, "Oh, it is just you!" He turned over and went back to sleep!

This should be the attitude of every believer who understands the great redemption of Christ.

The disciples knew the truth of this revelation. They knew that they were in a world dominated by the god of this world. They knew they had an enemy but they did not always cry out every time the devil harassed them.

Actually when Peter raised that woman from the dead, he did not go to her and say, "You spirit of death, leave her."

He knelt down and prayed. He got the mind of God. He turned to her and told her to get up. (Acts 9:40)

I believe in doing things the Bible way. It is not wrong to speak to the spirit of death. I am just telling you what the Bible says!

When Peter was put in prison, the saints commenced to have an all night prayer meeting. They ignored satan because they considered him defeated.

They assumed that what Jesus did was done! Jesus sent an angel to release Peter from the jail.

In Acts chapter four, they said, "And now, Lord, behold their threatenings: and grant unto thy servants, that with all boldness they may speak Thy Word, by stretching forth Thine hand to heal; and that signs and wonders may be done by the NAME OF THY HOLY CHILD, JESUS. And when they had prayed, the place was shaken where they were assembled together; and they were all filled with the Holy Ghost, and they spake the Word of God with boldness." (Acts 4:29-31)

They were Jesus-conscious!

As far as I can ascertain, the first mention of the devil in the Book of Acts, the New Testament church, is in chapter five. They had the mightiest revival going. I am sure they cast out demons. I am sure they rebuked the devil. I am sure that they had many things happen that are not recorded.

The early church paid very little attention to Mr. Devil. They moved with the assurance that he was defeated. They had absolute authority over him.

In Acts chapter five, Ananias and Sapphira lied to God. God revealed it to Peter.

"Peter said, Ananias, why hath satan filled thine heart to lie to the Holy Ghost, and to keep back part of the price of the land?" (Acts 5:3)

The first time satan stuck up his head, the Holy Ghost revealed what was being done and two people dropped dead! This is how much authority they had over satan's works.

The next time in Acts, chapter eight, a layman who later became an evangelist, went down to the city of Samaria, "Then Philip went down to the city of Samaria, and preached Christ unto them". (Acts 8:5)

Philip preached Christ! He preached the revelation of who Jesus is, what He did and who He conquered. He extolled the victory Christ gave us. He preached Jesus Christ is Lord. He preached the Kingdom of God. He preached about the Name of Jesus. Is it any wonder that such results were forth coming? Here is what the Bible says:

"And the people with one accord gave heed unto those things which Philip spake, hearing and seeing the miracles which he did. For unclean spirits, crying, with loud voice, came out of many that were possessed with them: and many taken with palsies, and that were lame, were healed. And there was great joy in that city." (Acts 8:6-8)

When Philip preached Christ, those demon powers subjected themselves to the Name of Christ. They admitted that Jesus was Lord. Jesus confirmed the Word. Philip was just a layman talking about Jesus and demon powers, screaming, came out of people!

I am convinced that the devil wants to get our attention and put on a show so that he can keep our attention on him all of the time.

Now, I realize also that you have to deal with demon powers. But if you will let them, they will keep you up all night. They want to talk to you. They want to harass you.

When the demons wanted to talk to Jesus, "He suffered not the spirits to speak to Him." (Mark 1:34)

Jesus is our example!

Jesus was dealing with an epileptic boy. The Bible says that He saw a crowd gathering together. He rebuked that spirit immediately and the spirit came out.

He would not allow the demon to put on a show for a curious crowd!

This is Bible truth!!

Thank God for preachers who are helping to set

the church free. Thank God for every special ministry. Thank God for those people who are patient and loving enough to work with people and counsel with them until deliverance is wrought.

BUT THE IDEAL WAY IS TO KNOW THE TRUTH AND CHASE THE DEVIL AWAY YOURSELF!!!

In Acts chapter thirteen, Paul and Barnabas were on a great missionary journey. The first encounter they had was with a sorcerer. (Remember that this is the Paul who wrote this great revelation of satan's defeat found in Ephesians.)

Paul and Barnabas went to preach the Word to the deputy of the country. "But Elymas the sorcerer (for so is his name by interpretation) withstood them, seeking to turn away the deputy from the faith. Then, Saul (Paul) *filled with the Holy Ghost . . .*" (Acts 13:8, 9)

That is the answer!

Jesus said, "I cast out demons by the Spirit of God." (Matthew 12:28) You can rant and rave all day long in your own strength. You need to let the Holy Ghost rise up in you.

. . . "Then Saul (Paul) filled with the Holy Ghost, set his eyes on him, and said, O full of all subtlety and all mischief, thou child of the devil, thou enemy of all righteousness, wilt thou not cease to pervert the right ways of the Lord?

And now, behold, the hand of the Lord is upon thee, and thou shalt be blind, not seeing the sun for a season. And immediately there fell on him a mist and a darkness; and he went about seeking some to lead him by the hand." (Acts 13:9-11)

Paul spoke to the *man;* not the demon. The man went blind, not the demon. This was what God told Paul to do!

We need to deal with each situation as the Holy Spirit directs us. If this had been some of us, we would have tackled the man and held him down until the demons came out. Why did they do differently? They listened to the Holy Ghost. We are to follow the direction of the Holy Ghost!

Jesus said, "I can of Mine own self do nothing." (John 5:30)

If Jesus couldn't, I surely cannot, nor can you. We are dependent upon the Holy Ghost.

Paul knew his power over satan! He preached the Gospel. He considered satan defeated. But he obeyed the Holy Ghost! When dealing with demonic powers, we need the mind of the Holy Spirit.

We need the Holy Ghost to flow through us more and more. We need him to saturate us throughout our very beings.

In Acts 16: 16-17 it says, "And it came to pass, as we went to prayer, a certain damsel possessed with a spirit of divination met us, which brought her masters much gain by soothsaying. The same followed Paul and us, and cried, saying, These men are the servants of the most high God, which show unto us the way of salvation." (Demons can talk religious.)

31

"And this did she many days . . ." (Acts 16:18)

Why didn't Paul cast out that spirit the first day? She harassed them many days. I do not know why Paul put up with her harassment for so many days.

He knew all about Jesus' promise that all believers have the power to cast out demons. (Mark 16:17) He also knew that, as Jesus, he could do nothing of himself. (John 5:30) He knew that he was to obey the Holy Ghost. He just put up with this harassment until he heard from God!

This shows us that Paul was just like you and me. He was human. He did not know everything automatically. He had to seek God.

Evidently the Spirit of God rose up in Paul. ". . . But Paul, being grieved, turned and said to the spirit, I command thee in the Name of Jesus Christ to come out of her. And he came out the same hour." (Acts 16:18)

Notice that the demon spirit left that woman that very moment. When Paul spoke with the authority of the Holy Ghost, it was done. That is the power of the Name of Jesus spoken at the direction of the Holy Ghost!!

You may minister as Paul in the power of the Holy Ghost. It may not look like anything has happened. But I want to tell you that when the Holy Ghost moves on you and you use the Name of Jesus, no matter what it looks like, know and believe that that demon left!

Acts 19:11, 12 says, "God wrought special

miracles by the hands of Paul: So that from his body were brought unto the sick, handkerchiefs or aprons, and the diseases departed from them and the evil spirits went out of them."

There was so much of the anointing of God on Paul that the things he touched became saturated with God's power. The evil spirits departed at the very scent of the aroma of God's Spirit.

WITCHCRAFT VS HOLY GHOST POWER

We have an Eskimo friend doing missionary work among the Eskimo tribes in Alaska near Siberia, Russia. This man was lost and without God. He was an alcoholic. Finally, he degenerated into what is known as a "crawling alcoholic". He could not walk. He simply crawled from room to room trying to exist on alcohol.

God led a Full Gospel minister again and again to share the love of Jesus of him. As this minister and his wife were there one day, they held this Eskimo in their arms and wept and prayed over him.

The Eskimo told me later that he asked himself, "Why would anyone weep over a stinking alcoholic like me?"

Then he said, "Maybe it is God in them Who cares for me."

As a result, he gave his heart to the Lord. Jesus saved him and delivered him from alcohol and he has been winning people to Jesus ever since.

He told me about his father. He said that his father was the leader of witchcraft in his family. He could name ten generations back those who had also headed the witchcraft cult in his family. For generations witchcraft had reigned in this family!

They were able to do powerful, supernatural things in the satanic spiritual realm. He said, "Brother Osteen, my father told me some startling things after I became a Christian."

His father was able to propel himself out of his body (astro-projection) and go in his spirit and perform supernatural evil deeds against people. He said that one day he decided to project himself out of his body in order to perform some evil work against a family who lived some distance away.

By the power of satan, he was able to go out of his body and go in his spirit to a certain village and a particular house. He said that this is what his father told him:

"As I approached this house in my spirit to perform my evil deeds, I noticed that in the spirit world the house was glowing as if on fire. I cautiously approached the place and looked inside. There were several people visiting this family. The visitors were all lit up like light bulbs. The people who lived in the house were dark, but the people who were visiting them were illuminated!

I found out later that there was a band of Christians visiting that had come to tell this lost family about Jesus.

I was unable to do any witchcraft in the presence of that great light, so I returned home."

Then the Eskimo said that his father turned to him and, with deep sincerity, he said, "Son, if Christians only knew the power and authority that they hold in the spiritual realm, they would never be afraid of satan and demon powers again!!"

Yes, we "shine as lights in the world," it says in Philippians 2:15.

"Ye are all the children of light, and the children of the day: we are not of the night, nor of the darkness." (I Thessalonians 5:5)

We do have power and authority, but we need knowledge of our abilities in the spirit realm.

In the spirit world, WE ARE LIGHTS!

The Psalmist David said, "Thou wilt light my candle; and the Lord my God will enlighten my darkness." (Psalms 18:28)

WE ARE DELIVERED FROM ALL DARKNESS!

Just as this Eskimo warlock was absolutely powerless in the presence of Jesus' Holy Ghost power through Spirit-filled Christians, so every other demonic activity is stopped when we use the Name of Jesus. Every form of the occult can be driven away in the Name of Jesus Christ. Every captive can go free! This Eskimo's son who was telling this story accepted Jesus Christ as his Lord and Savior. The power of witchcraft which had prevailed for ten generations was broken in his life by the Lord Jesus Christ!

You too can be delivered if you will do the following:

1. Confess to God that you have been involved in that which is wrong.

2. Renounce every form of the occult and witchcraft.

3. Burn or destroy every symbol, book or article that relates to the occult that is in your home or on your person.

4. Renounce your association and affiliation with satan and demonic forces.

5. Accept Jesus Christ into your heart as your Lord and Savior. After you have done this, command satan and demon forces to leave you in the Name of the Lord Jesus Christ and they will go. (Rom. 10:13; Rom. 10:9; Jn. 3:16, Acts 4:12; Jn. 3:3)

   James 4:7 says, "Resist the devil and he will flee from you." Mark 16:17 says, "In My Name you shall cast out devils."

6. Ask the Lord Jesus Christ to baptize you in the Holy Ghost. You will know this has happened when you begin to speak in other tongues. (Acts 2:4; Acts 1:8; Mk. 16:17; Mt. 3:11)

7. Find a good church where you can have fellowship with other believers.

8. Read and study your Bible EVERY DAY.

9. Pray and witness to others.

10. Rejoice daily that you are free! (II Cor. 5:17)

Christians need the instruction of the Holy Ghost. They need to know how to act on the truths found in God's Word. "God has given Jesus a Name that is above every name; that at the Name of Jesus, every knee shall bow of things in heaven, things in earth and things under the earth." (Philippians 2:9-10)

Jesus is the undisputed Lord of three worlds!!

The Name of Jesus prevails!!

Read and study the epistles in the Bible. God has given so much truth in the Word regarding your authority over demons and demon powers. The Word of God is your instruction.

It is ignorance that has weakened the body of Christ.

"You shall know the truth and the truth shall make you free." (John 8:32)

With the Name of Jesus Christ, you are as Christ in the face of demons. With the Name of Jesus, you are as Jesus physically standing in the face of the devil.

"We are not ignorant of the devil's devices." (II Corinthians 2:11)

The Word of God declares that we are not to be ignorant. But the sad thing today is that the church of the Living God has become ignorant. This is the reason that multitudes of Christians are tormented by demon harassment. Christians need to learn what God has given them in order to be victorious.

GIVE NO PLACE TO THE DEVIL

The Bible says, "Neither give place to the devil. Let no corrupt communication proceed out of your mouth, but that which is good to the use of edifying, that it may minister grace unto the hearers. And grieve not the Holy Spirit of God, whereby ye are sealed unto the day of redemption. Let all bitterness, and wrath, and anger, and clamour and evil speaking be put away from you, with all malice." (Ephesians 4:27, 29-31)

These sins in your life, unconfessed, will give satan a foothold.

While in Milwaukee, Wisconsin we ministered to a totally deaf woman. I said, "You foul spirits of deafness, in the Name of the Lord Jesus Christ, I command you to come out of these ears. I command these ears to be opened."

Instantaneously those spirits left her and she could hear perfectly. Everybody rejoiced!

The next night she returned to the service just as deaf as before. I called her up to minister to her. She was totally deaf. Again, I cast the devil out and commanded those ears to be opened. Again, she was delivered instantaneously! She could hear perfectly.

The third night she returned again totally deaf. Finally, I asked the pastor about her. He said, "Brother Osteen, do you see that man sitting beside her?"

I said, "Yes. I have noticed her husband with her in every service."

He said, "That is not her husband. She is living with that man in open adultery. The Lord has been dealing with her about renouncing this relationship, but she will not. She is able to hear until the moment she steps inside the house with him. As soon as she does, her deafness comes back on her. Because of her disobedience to God's laws, she is giving the devil a place in her life!"

She would not repent nor close the door to that demon power. She could not receive the power of God to stay free.

Jesus said to one man, "Sin no more, lest a worse thing come upon thee." (John 5:14)

Ephesians 6:11 tells us to "put on the whole armor of God that you may be able to stand against the wiles of the devil."

You can stand against all the wiles of the devil. You CAN do it. You can stand against everything the devil throws at you if you will put that armor on.

But, if you are lazy, worldly, unforgiving, bitter and will not listen to God's Word, you will be trapped by every snare of the enemy.

"God giveth more grace. Wherefore He saith, God resisteth the proud, but giveth grace unto the humble. Submit yourselves therefore to God. (That means God and the Word of God.) Resist the devil, and he will flee from you." (James 4:6-7)

When you are submitted to God, then when you resist the devil, he WILL flee in terror from you!

This means not only demons, but even the devil himself will flee from you.

"Casting all your care upon God; for He careth for you. Be sober, be vigilant; because your adversary the devil, as a roaring lion, walketh about, seeking whom he may devour: Whom resist steadfast in the faith . . ." (I Peter 5:7-9a)

This means you will not budge. You will not give an inch to the devil. You are immovable. You stand your ground.

This is the truth that makes you free!

THE STORY OF A SERPENT

When I was in Africa a few years ago, I had the privilege of visiting in the home of two of God's great missionaries. Their names are Brother and Sister J. R. Gschwend. They have done a mighty work over the past fifty years in Africa.

He tells of an experience that he had in the early days of his ministry in Africa. It is as follows: "It was on a hot Sunday afternoon that I was riding on horseback along a narrow winding path lined by large boulders to visit a certain outstation. Suddenly my horse stopped and refused to proceed. It seemed as if he scented something strange. It was at a place where the narrow path turned at a right angle behind one of the huge boulders that had long ago rolled down from the high mountains. I alighted from my horse to see what could be the cause of my horse's strange behaviour. Looking round the corner of the huge rock I saw a big snake lying in the middle of the path curled up, with its head under a loose flat stone. Being still a newcomer to Africa, and without any experience of snakes, I was puzzled to know what to do. The gruesome stories I had heard in the past about these dangerous and poisonous reptiles were enough to inspire fear in me. Since there was no other way to proceed on my journey, I had to make a plan to remove this snake, but did not know how, since I had no stick or weapon with me. It was a hot day and I presumed that the snake had placed its head underneath the flat stone for protection against the sun. The thought struck me that if I should cast a big stone and strike it with force upon the flat stone under which the snake's head lay, it would bruise its head and kill it. I picked up a heavy rock and moved towards the snake, almost trembling with fear, and wondering what would happen if I did not succeed in killing it on the spot. With all my strength I brought the big stone down upon the flat stone which broke in pieces, but to my surprise there was no movement in the snake, and I began to realize that the reptile had been dead for some time. Somebody else passing that way had bruised its head with the flat stone and left it there. I could not help but laugh over my foolishness and to think how I had been afraid of a dead snake, and on the other hand how courageous I had felt killing my first snake in Africa!

While I was still half ashamed of showing such fear and excitement over a dead snake, the still small voice of our Lord Jesus began to speak to me. 'Have I not long ago bruised the serpent's head on Calvary? Why then hast thou been so afraid, shaking and trembling over an enemy already conquered?"

'Yes, Lord Jesus, you have conquered sin, death and the grave and bruised the serpent's head, and I thank you for delivering us from the fear of death and hell,' I said. 'I shall henceforth fear no longer, but believe Your Word and let Your love which casteth out all fear rule in my heart'."

Yes, Another One has passed through this world. His Name is Jesus. When He came, He bruised the serpent's head. We do not have to do it again. IT IS ALREADY DONE!

We do not have to fear a totally defeated enemy! We have been given the right to use the mighty Name of the Lord Jesus Christ against the enemy.

I believe that the body of Christ is coming to understand their place of power and authority. You are a member of that body, so arise without fear and drive satan and demonic forces away from you!

Now go forth and deliver others as Jesus has commanded you to do!!!

IMPORTANT INSTRUCTIONS

The main purpose of this book is to help you individually as well as to enable you to help others in need. I would like to crystallize your thinking in certain areas so that you may get the maximum benefit from the truth that we have presented.

I am giving the following instructions because they are of vital importance. Let me encourage you follow them. As you do so, you will not only stay continually free from satan's influence and power, but you will be able to live a life of victory as you help others learn this truth.

ONE

Always talk about and confess who Jesus Christ is and what He has done for you through His death, burial, resurrection and ascension to the right hand of the Father. Don't be demon-conscious, but be Jesus conscious.

Don't always be talking about demons but always be talking and bragging on Jesus. Whatever you say about Jesus, He becomes that to you. He is to you what you say He is!

Boldly talk and confess the truth of the following scriptures:

"Jesus Christ is my Lord. He has been given a Name above every name that at the Name of Jesus every knee should bow, of things in heaven, and things in earth, and things under the earth; And that every tongue should confess that Jesus Christ is Lord, to the glory of the Father. (Philippians 2:9 & 10)

Jesus is seated at the right hand of the Father. He ever liveth to make intercession for me. (Hebrews 7:25) He has presented His holy blood in the presence of the Father and through that blood I can come boldly to the throne of grace, that I may obtain mercy, and find grace to help in time of need. (Hebrews 4:16)

Jesus Christ destroyed the works of the devil. (I John 3:8) He spoiled principalities and powers. He made a show of them openly, triumphing over them in it (the cross). (Colossians 2:15)

Satan is no longer lord of my life. Jesus Christ is Lord.

Jesus bore my sins, sicknesses and tasted my

death. (Isaiah 53:5; Hebrews 2:9) He bore the curse of the law in my place. (Galatians 3:13) He arose victorious and His victory is my victory!

The Father has delivered me out of the power of darkness and translated me into the kingdom of His dear Son. (Colossians 1:13)

I am a child of God, washed by the blood of Jesus and living in the kingdom of light."

TWO

Talk and confess freely about who you are in the Lord Jesus Christ and what you can do through His name and by the power of the Holy Spirit.

The Bible says that as in Adam all die, so in Christ all shall be made alive. (Romans 5:15)

You were a lost person in Adam, but thank God when you accepted Jesus Christ as your Savior and Lord you got out of Adam and in Christ.

II Corinthians 5:17 says, "Therefore if any man be in Christ, he is a new creature: old things are passed away; behold, all things are become new."

Boldly make the declaration that as a new creature "I can, in Jesus' Name, drive out demons."

"I can do all things through Christ who strengthens me." (Philippians 4:13)

"I have overcome satan because greater is He that is in me that he that is in the world. (I John 4:4)

I am washed by the blood of the Lord Jesus Christ. I am accepted in the Beloved. The Father loves me just like He loves Jesus. (John 17:26)

I have been given power to tread on serpents and scorpions, and over all the power of the enemy: and nothing shall by any means hurt me. (Luke 10:19)

Mark 16:17 & 18 tells me that because I am a

believer these signs shall follow me: In Jesus' Name I cast out devils; I speak with new tongues: I take up serpents, and if I drink any deadly thing, it shall not hurt me; I lay hands on the sick, and they shall recover.

I am the righteousness of God in Christ. (II Corinthians 5:21)

There is therefore, now no condemnation to me because I am in the Lord Jesus Christ. (Romans 8:1)

I have a heavenly position and kingly power because I bear the Name of the Lord Jesus Christ. (Ephesians 2:6)

All fear is gone and demons tremble at the sound of my footsteps because I am an ambassador of the Lord Jesus. (II Corinthians 5:20)

Jesus said that as a believer I could lay hands on the sick and they would recover. So, I boldly declare that I will lay hands on the sick and they will recover in Jesus' Name.

I am a deliverer. I step forth into the arena of human suffering with the mighty Name of Jesus to bring healing to the sick, deliverance to the captives and relief to the suffering."

You see, you must constantly confess these and other scriptures that describe who you are and what you can do in Christ Jesus. Never allow yourself to think nor talk otherwise for in doing so you would violate the great redemptive truths of the Word of God.

THREE

When demon powers come against you and satan himself attacks you, do not allow fear to make you magnify the situation. Do not begin to talk of all that satan and demon powers are trying to do to you. Do not rush excitedly and fearfully to the telephone to call everybody you know as though God had forsaken you and as if you were totally powerless.

All of us have battles. Satan and demon powers will always contest our rights. When this happens, we must realize our ability and power in the Name of Jesus Christ.

Jesus said, "In My Name you shall cast out devils." (Mark 16:17) This not only means cast out devils from others, but you will have the ability to drive demon forces away from yourself when they approach you.

The Bible clearly states that when the devil himself approaches you that if you will submit yourself to God and resist the devil then he will flee from you. (James 4:7) This means that he will actually run in terror from you. So you see, if the leader, satan himself, runs in terror when you use the Name of Jesus against him, how much more these demon powers will do so.

You rise up and speak to satan and demon powers yourself and freedom will be yours. Begin immediately to tell people how free you are, how wonderful Jesus is, and how powerful His Name is and you will enjoy the freedom that is yours whether you "feel" like it or not.

Now it is not wrong to call a prayer partner or some person who is close to you to agree with you and stand firmly against a satanic attack. Don't go to the extreme and feel that you have failed if you ask for help. The Bible says, "One can chase a thousand, and two put ten thousand to flight." (Deuteronomy 32:30)

The main thing is to refuse demons or satan any place in your mind, emotions, body or conversation. YOU must do the refusing. You must exercise your authority in the Name of the Lord Jesus Christ.

Never admit to yourself nor to anyone else that satan has dominion over you in any area of your life. On the contrary, always confess the lordship of Jesus in your life and your total mastery of satan and demon powers through His Name.

FOUR

When you deal with Christians who are truly oppressed by demon forces do so in a wise and scriptural way.

For instance, instead of pouncing upon them and beginning to shake them violently and scream at demons "In the Name of Jesus", why not take this approach: Let the Christian sit down and tell you what areas satan seems to have gained control. After listening, take the Word of God as presented in this book and throughout the Bible and patiently explain to this Christian his position, power, privileges and rights in the Lord Jesus Christ. Show him that Jesus Christ is now Lord and that He has given His Name and His power to every believer. Show him what Christ has done for him in breaking satan's lordship and power. Show him who he is in Christ.

Show this Christian who he is as a new creature in Christ and how the Bible explains his power and right and ability to use the Name of Jesus. Explain that satan has no rights to lord anything over him. Make it clear that they should no more tolerate satan's presence than they would a nest of rattlesnakes living within their clothing!

Let him humbly confess his sins which have allowed satan to become active in his life. Let him trust the blood of Jesus to make him totally free from all guilt and condemnation. Let the fellowship with God be restored through this confession. (I John 1:9)

Then, spend a time worshipping and praising God for His wonderful grace and mercy.

Now let this Christian begin to use the Name of Jesus and drive demon powers and satan himself away. Encourage him to read and study God's Word daily. Teach him to speak the Word of God with authority. Satan will flee, demon powers will go and this Christian will be totally free!

Now you have done more than help this Christian experience freedom. You have taught him how to stay free without depending on others. (It would also be helpful to put a copy of this book in his hand so that he can review these lessons.)